Dear Johen:

Our relationship is a
special one for me. From [illegible]
to here Estee - you've grown so
much and it's a pleasure to know
you and have you in my life

Warmest

Love

P.O.P.E

The Principles of
Prosperity Economics

P.O.P.E

The Principles of Prosperity Economics

The Path to Financial Wellness
Richard Pope, CAP

The Principles of
Prosperity Economics

This is a work of non-fiction. This publication is designed to provide accurate information on the subject matter covered. Client cases sited within are based on true cases but the names have been omitted or changed to protect client confidentiality. The information is not intended to replace any legal counsel or other professional directives. If professional services or advice or other assistance is required, the services of a professional should be sought.

ISBN: 1-57322-112-9

Library of Congress Control: On File With The Publisher

This book may be ordered by calling: (516) 516 677-6212

Business & Economics /Personal Finance

Printed in Canada

Cover Design: CGT Marketing

Dedicated to Patti

❦

*I feel deeply in my heart that this book
has to be dedicated to my wife Patti who
always has and continues
to support me in everything I do. She taught
me an important thought process
we should all learn as we grow our lives both personally
and financially – "Feel the fear and do it anyway."*

*Thank you Patti,
our lives are here because of
your ongoing love.*

Acknowledgements

Over the past twenty five years that I've been in this magnificent career there have been so many people that have guided me and helped me find my calling, that I simply cannot name them all without writing a separate chapter.

I believe in the power of mentorship and enjoy being a mentor to others today. This allows me to reflect those who have helped me become the person I am today. I can't name them all but just to name a few, John Anderson who taught me to think large, be the best at what you do and always care for the client first. The late Stan Closter who gave me my first break and extraordinary training in the financial services industry.

To the late Jeff Locker who opened my eyes to what the universe and love can provide if you let it and who introduced me to my current spiritual/business coach and friend Steve D'Annunzio.

To one of the most important people to ever enter my life, Steve D'Annunzio, who continues to teach me to lead with love, raise my awareness to engage my mission to help others and who through his love is the direct inspiration and driving force behind my writing this book.

To my friend Tim Foster who continually challenges me to grow and be the best and who has taught me his "mind travel" process.

To my staff, Celia, Denise and Olympia, who support me in so many ways.

To this book's editor, Sean Kennelly, who tirelessly made this dream become a reality.

Throughout my life, I have been blessed with the support of family and friends to achieve whatever it was that I wanted from life. Aunts, uncles and cousins alike. My father Louis who passed on too early to see my success, my mother Kaye who was always supportive and my brothers Butch and Joel for being there throughout.

To anyone and everyone who will gain something from this book.

Contents

Foreward & Author's Note

For close to four decades, I have had the opportunity to work with elite financial advisors throughout North America and around the world. One of the distinguishing characteristics of the best financial advisors is that they provide a model for their clients that leads to financial prosperity.

The average financial advisor focuses on methods to make money. The method may involve a particular product or investment approach. Too often, as Richard Pope so eloquently describes in this book, the allure of the product or approach does not lead to the results or outcome the client was expecting. In too many instances, the financial advisor appeals to fear or greed as the motivation to buy the proposed solution. The typical outcome is a disappointed client.

Elite advisors provide you with a model that describes why financial prosperity is important, how to get there and what it looks like when you arrive. The elite financial advisor recognizes that the starting point is your vision of what you want to achieve. Then, the advisor works with you to craft a strategy to realize your objectives.

Strategy is the alignment of your objectives with the resources and capabilities you have available and the opportunities and challenges the environment provides. The best advisors recognize that achieving and sustaining financial prosperity is a journey. As a Trusted Advisor, they accompany you each step of the way. They keep you on track by working with you to implement your plan.

An effective model is transformative. In a simple and profound manner, Richard Pope describes how to achieve financial prosperity. As an elite financial advisor, Richard Pope knows from experience the importance to his clients of a model for realizing their dreams. At a time when many people feel confused and uncertain about their financial wellbeing, the principles of prosperity economics provide a model for achieving financial security and independence as you define it.

This is a must read for those who want to achieve financial prosperity in these uncertain times.

Norm Trainor
Covenant Group

Introduction

July 30, 2012

As I sit in my New York offices, the stock market is in a temporary calm. I say "temporary" because last week the market endured three days of triple-digit losses for the first time since last September. Don't get me wrong. I'll certainly take every moment of sunshine and smooth sailing I can find, but as last week proves, I would be foolish to think that stormy seas are a thing of the past. In fact this could well be the eye of the next financial hurricane.

Forces beyond our control – the government, businesses, our fellow American citizens – can and will come together and create an atmosphere of panic. It's happened repeatedly over the past few years, causing the market to swing hundreds of points in a single day. So while the market basks in the glory of today's accomplishment, I know history will repeat itself. Market crashes have sadly become a part of our financial lives and not only are there more of them, but they are coming more often than ever leaving ruined businesses in their wake and the survivors increasingly numbed.

Just a few years ago the real estate bubble collapsed and from October 2007 to March 2009 the market lost over 53% of its value! We're still trying to recover from that slide and the damage it did. A few years before that the tech bubble burst and the market responded to the 9/11 terrorist attacks by losing nearly 38% of its value. Then there was the "flash crash" of May 2010 where nearly a trillion dollars of market value vanished in minutes. And who can forget Black Monday, October 19, 1987, where the market lost 22.6% of its value in one day!

The list of market crashes goes on and on. Throughout history whenever there's a rumor of war, there's a crash. Whenever there is a lack of confidence in the leadership of the nation, there's a slide. Now, with international financial interdependency, the panic has escalated to react to "any nation's problems" and the news loves to report on the doom and gloom. Whenever anything brings uncertainty into the picture, the market drops.

Yet the market doesn't run by itself (though it might seem that way with all the electronic trading that goes on these days). It's run by people. People who, more times than not, panic in the face of uncertainty. They can't help it! Like any human being, they fear loss and the market spirals downward with every panic attack.

Curiously, though, there are some people who have weathered these financial storms and have even gone on to increase their wealth. They experience growth in a time of loss. For them, volatility in the market does not dictate their actions. They don't spend their time chasing the gains. They don't spend their time worrying about the market losses. They spend their time working, playing, and enjoying an outstanding quality of life.

So what's their secret? How do they find profit where others find loss? And how do they insulate themselves, their businesses and their loved ones from the harsh realities of moody market swings? It all has to do with how they think and what philosophies they employ on a daily basis. They're not so ego-driven to think they can change the market. But anyone can change how they think and thinking is the key to what I call Prosperity Economics.

I remember sitting in my office just last August when the market took a nasty 500-point plunge. I'm sure the phones in most financial advisors' offices were ringing off the hook with clients worried about the declining value of their portfolios. My phones were silent. And that's what I'd call a "ringing" endorsement of the Principles of Prosperity Economics.

Richard Pope

Chapter 1

Blinded By The Truth

As a financial advisor it's my job to safeguard my clients' money and at the same time give it every opportunity to grow. This can be a delicate balancing act for some advisors, filling their hearts, minds, and client portfolios with anxiety and fear. They and their clients ride a daily emotional roller coaster as they chase the market.

Other voices out there try to paint convincing pictures of financial triumph and big gains. Some may even tell you how easy it is and how "anyone can do it." Though I'm sure there are exceptions to every rule, armchair quarterbacks are not the kind of people you hand the ball to when the outcome of a big game or your financial future is on the line.

Then there are still others who treat investing like a form of legalized gambling, constantly searching for the next jackpot growth fund or real estate development, hungry for an influx of wealth that will finally insulate them from the winds of financial reversal.

Sadly, they are all caught up in a maelstrom of their own making and it all has to do with perspective. How we see things influences our every decision and colors our judgment.

Such is the case in the tale of The Blind Men and the Elephant. Originating in India, the story is found in many parts of Asia with slight variations. It goes something like this.

The Blind Men and the Elephant

There were once six wise men from India. They were known as the wisest of the wise, great men of learning and wisdom. Yet they relied heavily on their senses in the pursuit of knowledge for they were all blind.

One day they were brought to examine the Elephant, a creature they had never before had the courage to approach. They had heard all about its great size and strength. They knew the rich nobles often rode elephants, for it kept them beyond the reach of hungry tigers that crouched in the tall grass, ready to kill unwary travelers.

As they were led to the Elephant, the men decided that they would discard the descriptions they had heard and decide for themselves what an elephant was truly like. The six blind men were placed around the elephant and each one took turns feeling the beast and giving a report of what he experienced.

The First Man walked up to the Elephant and stumbled, falling into the side of the creature. "God bless me!" the First called out, "But an Elephant is very much like a wall!"

The Second Man reached out and felt the Elephant's tusk. "Ho, what have we here?" the Second cried out. "So very round and smooth and sharp! It is clear to me that this wonder called an Elephant is very much like a spear!"

The Third Man walked towards the animal and caught hold on the Elephant's squirming trunk with his hands. "I see," said the Third as he wrestled to hold the trunk, "The Elephant is very much like a snake!"

The Fourth Man reached out his eager hand and felt the Elephant's wrinkled and thick leg. "What this wondrous beast is most like is very plain to me," the Fourth proclaimed. "It is clear enough that the Elephant is very much like a tree!"

The Fifth Man, who touched the giant creature's ear said, "Even the blindest man can tell what this beast most resembles. Who can deny the fact that this marvel of an Elephant is very much like a fan!"

At last the Sixth Man reached with outstretched hands and latched upon the beast's tail as it swished from side to side. "Say what you will but I must confess," the Sixth proudly announced, "This Elephant feels very much like a rope!"

Loud and long did each of the men dispute the findings of the others, for they had each experienced the truth for themselves. How could anyone tell them otherwise? So they argued all day and into the late evening hours, unwilling to bend or even consider the other men's findings.

Each knew they were right and yet they were all wrong. For an Elephant was more than just a side, a tusk, a trunk, a leg, an ear, or a tail. It was a complete beast made of marvelous parts. And despite all their wisdom and learning, they just couldn't see it.

Notice the blind men were not poor, ignorant souls. They were "great men of learning." Yet their perspective blinded them to the truth. The whole truth. They couldn't connect the dots. Each man was right and yet they got it wrong.

How did they get it wrong? Each had a well-informed feel for their part of the elephant but that truth did nothing to help them make an accurate judgment of the entire beast. They really couldn't help themselves. Their thinking was flawed and based on a partial truth. Some may have even sensed that there was more out there than just their part of the elephant but denied such thoughts for fear that they might look foolish or weak.

Sounds a lot like the world of wealth accumulation to me. So much of it is interrelated but so few connect the dots or realize that the pieces are all part of the same beast. Sometimes we even believe that our part is the only part that's important. The problem is the market ignores the other parts. It's a living, breathing animal and all the other parts continue to work as they always have and sad is the investor who finds out a little too late that there is more to the elephant than just the tail.

Paradigm Blindness

"The Chinese use two brush strokes to write the word
"crisis." One brush stroke stands for the word "danger";
the other for the word "opportunity."

John F. Kennedy

How we "see" things makes all the difference in our lives. Where one man sees a crisis, the other man sees an opportunity. You can take a glass of water and where one person sees a glass that is half full, another person will see it as half empty. Some might see this as a simple case of optimism vs. pessimism but it's more than that.

We each bring to our lives a set of beliefs and ideas that have been shaped by a variety of forces – some beneficial and some harmful and all of them instructive. Some forces teach us love and understanding. Some forces teach us doubt and prejudice. Those life lessons are part of every decision we make and they can cloud our vision and distort the truth.

For instance, a woman may look out her kitchen window day after day, watching her neighbor hang laundry out to dry on a clothesline. It's a sight to behold because as often as her neighbor washes her clothes, they never seem to get clean. There are always spots and smudges on the clothes. The woman shakes her head and thinks to herself, "What an idiot! Doesn't she know how to wash clothes? Is she even using soap?" Then one day the woman looks out the window as she usually does and to her surprise, the neighbor's laundry is immaculate. There's not a spot or smudge to be found. "Looks like she finally figured out how to wash laundry," she thinks. Then her husband comes in and proudly announces that he just finished washing all the windows in the house. And the woman realizes how clouded her vision had been.

Like the woman in the house, we often allow our circumstances to cloud our vision. We think we see things clearly but are totally unaware of the spots and smudges on our own windows. As a result, we misjudge things and not seeing the truth is as good as being blind. That's what I call paradigm blindness.

What, you ask, is paradigm blindness? A paradigm is the collection of beliefs and ideas that form your window on the world. If that window is clouded to any degree, we are blind to the truth. We can't see it all. We may see part of it, but it clouds everything including our interpretation and it causes us to believe that the neighbor next door is a clothes-washing moron. Based on that "view" we say or do things and often times, as in the case of the woman in the house, we end up feeling pretty foolish when we discover the truth.

It's nothing to be embarrassed about. Paradigm blindness strikes us all. It's a disease we all suffer from; at least to the degree that we insulate ourselves from outside influences and refuse to accept the possibility that our windows may be dirty. "I can see just fine," we tell ourselves and in our own hubris we actually think we're protecting our view from contaminating influences that might warp the truth. In reality, our view is no better than the blind men. And sometimes we only see what we want to see or what we hope to see and ignore the truth that's right in front of our face. We really can't help it though, because one of the things that cloud our view the most is fear.

The F.E.A.R Factor

If there's one evil in this world that has done more to ruin lives and devastate wealth, it is fear. If you ever want to get to the root cause of just about every crime ever committed, it's pretty much rooted in fear. If you want to understand why ignorance runs rampant in this world of ours, you can point the finger squarely at fear. If you wonder why some people fail to reach their full potential in life – hello, fear.

So what is fear, really? Fear can be summed up in its letters: **F**alse **E**vidence **A**ppearing **R**eal. Or try Future Events Appearing Real. Either way, you have a belief in something that does not exist, has not existed, and most likely will never exist at all. And we base so many of our actions on non-existent, non-factual events or evidence? That's insane. And that is what we are when we allow ourselves to get caught up in fear. Let me share a story from Asia about a young boy who wanted to become a Buddhist monk.

The Boy and the Board

Once there was a boy who approached a monastery, desiring to enter and become a monk. He was greeted by the head monk or abbot and taken to a small room where a shallow pool covered most of the floor. The bottom of the pool was littered with human bones and the boy shrunk back in dread at the sight. Above the pool lay a single, narrow board.

The abbot explained that he would be happy to accept the boy into the monastery provided he could pass a test. His task? To walk across the plank above the pool to the other side. Seems easy enough, thought the boy, though the bones bothered him and the board was a bit narrow.

The abbot motioned to the pool before them and told the boy that the pool was not water, but acid. The bones at the bottom of the pool belonged to people who had failed the test and fell to a horrible death in the acid. The boy shuttered at the thought of such a painful end. Seeing his concern, the abbot asked if he still wanted to enter the monastery. Despite his fears, the boy agreed to complete the task in one week.

To practice for his test, the boy took a narrow board like the one over the pool of acid and placed it on some rocks above the ground. He practiced day and night. Though he often fell, he kept trying and by the end of the week he mastered the task. Not only did he not fall, but he could do it blindfolded while walking backwards!

The abbot was impressed with the young boy's ability and determination. He knew the boy had the skill to pass the test. Yet when it came time to perform the task, the boy looked over the pool of acid and the bones and trembled with anxiety. He knew if he fell off the board, he would die. He broke into a sweat at the thought of failure. For a moment he considered quitting and walking away, but he was determined to win entry into the monastery. So he stepped onto the board and began to cross.

He trembled as he took each step. Then as he reached the midpoint, his fears rushed in. He looked down at the bones, lost his balance and fell!!

The boy braced himself for the pain but as he splashed into the acid nothing happened. No burning, no pain, just... wet. He jumped up and scrambled out of the shallow pool in a panic.

The abbot laughed!

The boy was confused. The abbot smiled and explained that the pool was just water and that the bones were the remains of people who had died naturally and were only there for the test.

"Do not worry, my boy," the abbot added. "Many have failed the test, but all have learned the lesson."

"What is the lesson?" the boy asked.

"There is no truth in fear," the abbot replied. "As you started across the pool, you knew that if you fell you might die a horrible death. But you did not. That which you feared was a lie. That lie became more powerful than the truth. You knew you could walk across that board and yet you fell. And now you know the lesson. Welcome to the monastery!"

Can you see the truth? Fear is never based on facts. It's always based on fiction. It's based on little stories we tell ourselves when we don't have all the facts and it's all in our heads. And if we're not careful it can rule our lives.

We live in a very fearful society. Whenever the weatherman predicts a major snowstorm, everyone is afraid they might be stranded without bread and milk. So people rush out to the grocery stores and empty the shelves. We worry that our children will make poor choices and experience some negative consequences, so we try to control them and remove any opportunities for them to choose for themselves. (Is it just me or has the population of control freaks in this world just exploded over the past few years?) Even the politicians are afraid, so they make every attempt to silence anyone who disagrees with their point of view and we find our government locked in partisan politics where compromise is a dirty word.

I watch fear take hold of the financial markets on a daily basis. It's the engine behind most all of the moody market swings. I wouldn't be surprised if the stress from such a volatile market is responsible for a good chunk of the nation's medical expenses and health issues.

Fear is epidemic. We seek security instead of opportunity. We settle for mediocrity instead of uncommon achievements and we do all we can to insulate ourselves from the financial storms and hope to survive. So we gamble and chase the market. And it all fuels what I call Scarcity Economics.

Chapter 2

The Money Hunt - Scarcity Economics

We live in a world of limited resources. Despite the "unlimited" data packages offered by the cell phones companies (or at least they used to offer them) and season passes to your favorite water park with unlimited visits, there is a limit to all resources and the more limited the resources, the greater the price to acquire such resources.

The one resource no one ever seems to get enough of is money. No matter how much or how little you earn, it never seems to be enough. "We can't afford it" is a phrase uttered in more households than we care to admit and it stems from an outlook clouded by scarcity.

There Isn't Enough

One of the great fears that runs rampant through our society is the worry that there isn't enough, that somehow it will all disappear and there won't be any tomorrow. How else can you explain why many people pile their plates sky high at an "All-You-Can-Eat" buffet. It's like they think the kitchen is going to run out of food and if they don't get it all now, somehow they'll miss out. That is scarcity thinking on display.

For an even better example, take a look at someone like Bernie Madoff. The guy was rolling in dough from all his scams and yet he kept looking for more money and more people he could take money from. Why? It just wasn't enough. It would never be enough because with each new bundle of cash came the fear that there might not be more. So off Bernie went in search of more clients he could tap for more money.

Believe it or not, there are a lot of people out there like Bernie Madoff. Their fears drive their belief that there will never be enough. It drives them to do things they once thought wrong and to rationalize their "need" for it. I mean, no criminal ever thinks they've done anything wrong. They have a list of excuses and "reasons" a mile long for every crime they've ever committed, but at the end of the day it's just not right. And it's rooted in scarcity thinking.

Scarcity thinking is a tool used by marketing and sales people on a daily basis to close deals. They manipulate people into taking action today by making them feel as if they might not have the same opportunity tomorrow. We've all see the tactic before. "The first 50 callers will get our free guide to happiness" (right, if only it was that easy). "Hurry, limited time offer!" How about a sale for "one-day only!" And who can resist "while supplies last." Black Friday sales during the Thanksgiving holiday are filled with such catch phrases. So are car dealerships ("What do we have to do to make this happen today?"). Does it work? All the time.

Chasing the Gains

Scarcity thinking has invaded every aspect of our lives. How else can you explain the explosion of day traders and even professional brokers who spend every waking hour (and probably a few while they sleep) searching for the next golden stock, bond, money market fund or annuity? They're driven by fear and greed to find the golden goose that they can spin to their clients (or themselves). Even stockholders are part of the equation as they demand higher profits every year.

This frantic activity is what I call chasing the gains and it produces financial insanity on every level. It turns the markets into institutionalized gambling halls full of high rollers, cheap thrills and lots of smoke & mirrors.

And when there are no gains to be found, the truth is twisted and presented in such a way as to paint a rosy picture of whatever financial product, service or fund they're selling.

For example, a mutual fund could hide losses and actually appear to have a high rate of return depending on how they present the math. Let's say you invested $1000 in year one and that year the fund was phenomenally successful and doubled your money, an unheard of 100% rate of return. So at the end of year one you'd have $2000. If you lost 50% in year two, you'd be back to $1000. If they had another 100% rate of return in year three, you'd be back to $2000. And if the fourth year was another 50% loss, then you'd be back to your original $1000 at the end of year four.

So you invested $1000 at the beginning of year one, gained 100%, lost 50%, gained 100% and lost 50%. Averaging those four years, the fund could say they have a 25% rate of return and not lie. But how much more money did you make? None. Why? Because the losses hurt you more than the gains helped you. Of course some advisors would simply tell you that the average is "weighted" but the money doesn't lie. There were no gains at the end of the four year period.

Scarcity thinking strikes again!

For as long as most can remember, America has been a prosperous nation. It has often been called the land of opportunity, but our country has drifted into a mire of compromise and greed. We lust after that which is not our own and encroach on the property and profit of others at every opportunity. And when you must constantly watch for those that might take advantage of you, the financial marketplace is filled with fear and instability.

You have no idea how much your stock portfolio or mutual fund will be worth tomorrow. So you panic. That fear in turn creates more panic-stricken people and the market makes a huge swing. Then the reactions to the swing feed into the financial frenzy.

Financial Paralysis

As a result, small businesses become paralyzed, unsure how the market could affect them. So they do nothing. Working men and women worry, knowing they could lose what little they've been able to invest. So they do nothing. And people on the verge of retirement are scared to death. It's too late for them to make a strategic move out of the market. If they do, they could suffer great losses. So they do nothing. Even the wealthy realize taxes may change as a result of the market shifts, so they don't want to do anything either. So instead of taking action, they freeze and nothing changes for them either.

The cycle goes on and on with fear creating uncertainty which creates more fear and more uncertainty. That's Scarcity Economics in action. It's a vicious cycle but you don't have to be the victim here. You can do something! Unlike the blind men in the first story, you can learn to see the whole elephant. But it will require you to open your eyes a bit and maybe clean the glass of your kitchen windows, because we allow a LOT of smudges and smears to distort our vision of the truth.

Misinformation

Misinformation is one of the biggest imaginable obstacles to true wealth and a huge product of scarcity thinking. We're taught all kinds of myths about money growing up. Some of it comes from your parents. As a child you'd lobby your folks for the latest toy or trinket at the store and you'd hear stories like "we can't afford it" or "money doesn't grow on trees." You fill in the blank here. We all heard the same stories and stories feed Scarcity Economics.

Where do these stories come from? From the blind men on every side of the elephant and they're all absolutely convinced that they have the corner on the truth. I like to call it hype, but it's information based on partial truths that have been mass-marketed to everyone in America and beyond. The problem? People believe them.

You would think living in today's skeptical society that people might second guess the information they hear or see, but as the famous showman P.T. Barnum once said, "There's a sucker born every minute!".

For example, before the big real estate bust a few years back there were huge real estate investments around the country where thousands of condos were being built in places like Miami. Some of the huge companies building these condos were looking for more capital. So what they did was go to a bunch of investment bankers, who went to common citizens and said, "Why aren't you diversified in real estate?". The common citizens said, "I don't know anything about real estate." The bankers said, "Look, the condos are going up! There are all these European buyers. They're selling like hotcakes. You'll make tons of money!"

So without any protection, without any real evidence or assurance that if anything went wrong in the economy, they'd still get paid, these people leveraged their savings to chase a storied rate of return, because they were afraid if they didn't act they would lose out on the really big money. They made an investment based in fear without any personal investigation and without any understanding of the risk involved. They bought into the story they were being told and yet the whole deal was built on hype!

You get hype any time you walk into a car dealership. The salesmen are there to sell you a car, even if you have no intention of buying. They spin it any way they can so they can make the sale. Whether they realize it or not, people from all walks of life are all selling themselves and/or their firms or companies. They are all chasing the same almighty buck from every client, so they all have their spin their products and services as they sell their own part of the elephant. They loudly proclaim they have the answer to all your financial woes. They say they have your back. But do they?

They'll use your ignorance to fuel your fear, hoping to make a sale. "The market's declining, it's time to buy!" they'll urge. "The window of opportunity is closing!" they'll proclaim. "This company could be the next big thing," they'll say. Whatever it takes to move you to action and separate you from your money. Now not all financial professionals are like this, but can you tell what their agenda is and whether they're looking out for your best interests or theirs?

Of course some of the masters of hype are people I call celebrity advisors. You know these people. You know their names. You've probably read their books or watched their TV or radio programs. There's a reason that the media is often referred to as the entertainment business. It is designed to entertain and it is most definitely a business. And they only make money when they sell advertising or products such as get-rich-quick CDs or beat-the-market DVDs. Whether or not what these advisors preach is the "truth" is immaterial as long as it brings in the bucks.

Unfortunately their one-size-fits-all financial advice doesn't always pan out and how can it? Everyone has a very specific financial situation. And who pays the price when their advice doesn't pan out? You do.

Days before Bear Sterns went belly up, the host of CNBC's Mad Money, Tim Cramer, told the audience that he felt Bear Sterns was still a great investment. At the time it might have seemed like sound financial advice, but he was wrong. Those who listened and thought this to be the truth paid a heavy price. And despite this and other similar "advice" from other celebrity advisors that fails to pan out, people still don't remember that these advisors are really just entertainers. They are even referred to as "on-air talent" within the media. Do you really want "talent" advising you where to put your nest egg?

When these celebrities appear on a commercial telling us how easy it is to profit in the stock market, that the market "always comes back so hang in there," why do you believe them? What if a well-known neurosurgeon advertised his new internet website where he would walk you through do-it-yourself brain surgery? "It's easy," he'd say. "Anyone can do this! It's a no-brainer!" (pardon the pun). Would you even remotely consider trying it? On someone you cared about? No way! Neither would I. You'd want to sit down with a qualified, experienced professional that you had carefully researched, a doctor trusted by his profession and perhaps by your close friends to do the job right. Getting sound financial guidance is no different. It comes from an experienced, insightful professional, not an infomercial.

Opinion vs. Fact

It astounds me how easily people are mesmerized by supposed experts who tout their opinions as if they were facts, yet it happens over and over again. It's not uncommon for celebrity "advisors" to buy, then promote a certain stock to their viewers or clients. Finally, once they've artificially driven the stock price up, they sell and make a nice profit. Anyone watching this trend can testify to how often this type of scenario plays out. People who listened know what a mistake it was to follow the celebrity's "advice" to begin with, but why is it that no one seems to learn their lesson? You guessed it, scarcity thinking.

Another thought process that always amazes me is: "I asked my friends about this and they said it's no good." When I hear this I have to ask them: "Would you mind if I asked who these friends are? What are their professional credentials? Why are their opinions anything more than just that?" and "Is your life identical to their lives?". It's always amazing that people gravitate to the easy way out rather than taking the time to become educated for their own benefit.

It's like the boy walking over the pool that appeared to be filled with flesh-eating acid. Fear of the acid and the pain it might bring kept him from realizing the truth and actually caused him to tumble and fall. Likewise, many people base their financial decisions on opinions and not facts. Inevitably they fall. And we find opinions paraded as fact almost everywhere we go.

Net worth? Opinion. Real estate appraisal? Opinion. Why else do banks require some form of down payment on a property? They recognize the appraisal for what it is – an opinion. Nothing more. What about a doctor's diagnosis? Opinion. A very educated opinion based on facts – but have all the right facts been discovered, facts that give a complete picture of the situation at hand? Until that time, it's a judgment call. What about your own hopes and dreams? Do you base your actions today on something that hasn't even happened yet? That's just another example of making decisions based on opinion and fear.

Honestly, we can't help it. Most financial decisions are based on the assumption that our current income level will increase or at least stay the same. What if we lose some major clients? What if we're fired from a lucrative position? What if we get sick and lose the ability to bring in the same income we're accustomed to? So our opinions really shape our decision-making. Yet we have to realize that basing our decisions on opinions leads to uncertainty and fear and feeds right into scarcity thinking.

Many of these opinions are handed down from father to son, mother to daughter like family heirlooms and that, to me, is frightening. One of the grand old traditional opinions which have been handed down from generation to generation is a group of old financial guidelines known as Accumulation Theory.

Old Rules - Accumulation Theory

Nothing has had a greater impact on the current financial mindset of our nation (and to some degree, the world) than the Great Depression of the 1930s. People lost their jobs, their businesses, and their homes and, in the process, their positive outlook on life. Fear etched itself into the hearts of every man, woman, and child. That fear is pervasive throughout the baby boomer generation and is still being passed onto the younger generations.

Ever wonder why so many of us are reluctant to throw away broken appliances or why we save every magazine or newspaper that we've ever subscribed to? Ask any hoarder and they'll tell you that "you never know when you might need it." Really? For some it's a security blanket and even if their house burns to the ground, they'll actually go out of their way to fill their new home with stuff that they've rescued from garage sales and thrift stores.

Ever wonder why America has an obesity epidemic on its hands? Look to the Great Depression where "clean your plate" became a mantra. In fact, some people were so worried that they might not eat again that they ate everything they could at one sitting. Today, we live in a land of abundance and still feel the need to eat everything we can at one sitting.

"Save for a rainy day" was a guiding principal for those shell-shocked by the economy of the day. For most that meant sticking their money in a safe place and sitting on it. Though times have changed, people are still stuck in this mentality today and act as if they're trying to dodge losses by doing nothing to grow their money. And out of those that choose to save, few save enough for their futures. So why are today's American's saving so little yet gambling so much? The answer: Accumulation Theory.

Accumulation Theory is an old way of thinking where accumulating money or things will somehow make us more prosperous. It's why most multi-million dollar lottery winners are poor and penniless in record time. It's why star athletes are broke within the first year or two after their professional careers are over. Did accumulating more money or stuff help them?

In his book, The Prosperity Paradigm, author Steve D'Annunzio compares Accumulation Theory to the copper wire you use to bring electricity into your home. You can accumulate piles of copper wiring in your garage, but until you hook it up to a source of energy there will be no electricity in the house. No power.

Money operates in the same way. Many people falsely believe that if they accumulate more money and stash it away in a bank account, they'll be safe and secure. If banks operated in this manner, they'd never make a dime. In fact, they'd go broke since there would be no money to pay their staff to take your money and store it in the bank vault. There wouldn't even be a security guard to protect the vault. Sure they keep some cash on hand, but it doesn't sit around collecting dust and neither should your money.

Like the copper wire in the house, money is not the power source. It is a conduit of power or value. The more value you give to the world around you – whether it's business, your personal life, etc. – the more value flows back to you in the form of true wealth, relationships, and power.

So if you're tired of what you're getting right now in business or life, start thinking differently. Scarcity thinking is self-serving and outdated. As sure as the sun shines, it will destroy your future growth and happiness. Is that really what you want? Because there is so much more. You just have to be willing to embrace a new way of thinking, a way that is based in facts and real knowledge.

Ignorance

> *"Ignorance prevails when a person is unwilling to grow out of their comfort zone, and is often accompanied by a deep stubbornness to adapt and change."*

Steve D'Annunzio, *The Prosperity Paradigm*

Ignorance is more than just a dirty word we sling around to describe a lack of knowledge. Ignorance describes a condition where not only is there a lack of knowledge, but there is a real fear of it. As a result you end up living life with a set of beliefs that are flawed or false. Change is the enemy and "if it isn't broke, don't fix it" is a way of life. But how do you know if it's really not broke? Can we really stand still and resist change? And what happens when we do?

If we look at the world of nature we see an interesting truth. Everything in nature is doing one of two things: it is either growing or dying. There is no middle ground. When flowers bloom in your garden at home they are either growing or they are shriveling, having served their purpose in beautifying the world around them. Flowers don't fight the change. They can only fulfill their purpose and move on. They can't halt the process.

We are much like flowers. We have a purpose and we can either grow to fulfill that purpose or die, but we can't resist the change. We can lie to ourselves, but when we are not growing, we're dying. Whether that process is emotional, intellectual, physical or financial doesn't matter. We either grow and bloom or we decay and die. Ignorance breeds inevitable decline. It's that simple. And that's just another hard-learned aspect of the scarcity mindset.

Emotions + Bad Info = Financial Disaster

> *"If you can't control your emotions,*
> *you cannot control your money."*

Warren Buffet

We are emotional creatures. We can't help it. It's just who we are. We attach emotions to just about everything. Why is comfort food called comfort food? Because it evokes a pleasant memory based on taste and smell. That memory may be that of a loving parent at home as he or she dishes up a healthy spoonful of mashed potatoes and gravy, or that of a lover who prepared a special dish and every time we eat it, our minds are saturated with happy memories of the experience.

What about when you hear a favorite song of yours? You know, the one that you heard on a happy occasion or when you first fell in love? Just hearing the song brings back a flood of memories and a smile to your face. We even put photos or art on the walls of our homes and offices to evoke emotions and feelings. And we all love the kind of movie that gives us such a great emotional experience that we go back and watch it over and over again. We love emotions – at least the positive ones and maybe the occasional "safe" scare from a fast-paced thrill ride or a scary novel.

These are all reactions to things that we experience in the world around us, and they can be enjoyable. However reacting to things in an emotional way can be harmful. Just look at the classic knee-jerk reaction. A knee-jerk reaction is something that we do without thinking based on past experience. It's unconscious and can be a dangerous thing when it comes to your financial decisions.

Everyone has some emotional connection with money. If you grew up in humble circumstances, you may do everything you can now to save money and accumulate enough funds to insulate you from ever having a financial worry, only to have half your money disappear in a bad real estate deal (who knew the bubble would burst, right?) or the next big bull stock market. Or you may be a spender because your parents tried to micromanage you earnings as a teenager and, being a rebellious youth, you showed them by spending it all. So when your significant other recommends saving or investing for the future you think: Save? Future? Eat, drink, and be merry for tomorrow we die!

That may be a bit of an exaggeration, but you get the point. Money can make people crazy. It breaks up marriages, friendships, and launches a legion of lawsuits. Combine that insanity with bad financial information or opinions and you have a recipe for financial apocalypse. It's hard enough to make good financial decisions with good information when we're calm and rational.

Solid, reliable information about money and investments is critical to success when it comes to financial planning. Yet our world is filled with bad information, bad advice, and bad examples of how to handle your hard-earned cash. Throw in the slightest emotional element to the mix and voila – you have a certified mess on your hands. Here's a nightmare scenario:

You study the stock market like a pro and decide to become a day trader so you can reap the benefits or your vast knowledge and internet search abilities. I've worked with many clients like this. You ignore the advice of your financial advisor because you "read the trends" better than they do. Or do you? So you jump in and make a substantial buy on a company you heard is on the cusp of a new technology. The problem? The information you're acting on is old news to the rest of the financial community and they begin selling in droves. You think they're foolish so you continue to sink money into the stock (dollar cost average, right?) and by the end of the day your investment is worth half what you paid for it. Your emotion (pride) got the better of you and you end up paying a hard price for your lack of knowledge.

It all adds up! The financial equation became your reality. Emotion (in this case pride) plus Bad Information (who knew that the information you had was old news) equaled Disaster! There is no escaping the deadly combination. We've all fallen into the trap. The key now is to avoid making poor financial decisions. Your financial future depends on it!

So…are you in it for the long haul or are you chasing the quick gain? Can you delay gratification? Can you control your emotional knee-jerk reactions? Who's steering your ship? Fear or Fact?

Is The Sky Falling

With so much fear, bad advice, misinformation, and just plain risky business, is it any wonder that most investors feel like they're on an emotional roller coaster every day? And even on days when the financial prognosticators see sunshine and blue skies, the voice of fear says another market crash is just around the corner. So you take steps to protect yourself. You accumulate as much wealth as possible and lock it up at the finest bank or portfolio you can find and you sit on it, hoping to avert disaster. Then the bank goes belly up! Or along comes a Bernie Madoff who runs off with half or more of your wealth. Or a tsunami wipes out your investment condos and you find out that the insurance policy doesn't cover water damage from a tidal wave. Or, worse yet, the value of the dollar suddenly plummets and the price of everything doubles overnight.

The list of potential disasters goes on and on and so does your fearful mind as it races to the next fright-filled conclusion all based on fiction and lies.

Is the sky falling? It all depends on your point of view and your paradigm. If you're the blind man holding the tail of the elephant, you might come to the conclusion that an elephant is skinny with very little muscle or meat on its bones. And while that may be true of the tail, you're missing the rest of the elephant. Your windows are dirty and you're allowing your fears to knock you off balance financially. Then when you fall and find out that the fears really were fiction, you get back up and begin again and the vicious cycle of scarcity economics begins anew.

Aren't you tired of basing your decisions on the pundits' preaching and the whims and fears of others? Wouldn't you sleep better at night if you ignored the latest market report? One thing's for certain – nothing will change until you decide to change.

There is a better way to live life, a way that will allow you to sleep peacefully every night. It's time to clean your dirty windows and get on a path to financial wellness where financial knee-jerk reactions are a thing of the past and knowledge is king. It's time to see the whole elephant. It's time for Prosperity Economics!

Chapter 3

True Wealth Building - Prosperity Economics

Today's health and wellness market is huge but despite all the hoopla over being physically fit and eating right, we have a serious problem with obesity. Even with all the facts in front of us, many of us choose to live an unhealthy lifestyle. We complain how the diets are too restrictive, the required exercise is too hard, and that it's too expensive to be physically fit. So, we ignore the facts and hope they'll go away…even though we know it might shorten our life span. This has created the birth of a new America – the fast food nation where it's all easy.

That is the real challenge to Prosperity Economics or any new way of thinking: change. It's hard to undo years of habit. So as I unveil the Principles of Prosperity Economics (or P.O.P.E. for short), remember that there is a screaming, anti-change demon inside that will try to undermine your every step down this new path. Don't listen to him (or her)!!

The path to prosperity is not covered in rose petals; it's paved with hard work, self-discipline, persistent effort, and uncommon knowledge. For some the way may not be easy, but know that it's worth every step. And know that anyone can walk this path, including you!

Wealth Building: Luxury or Expense

Building wealth is never easy and it never happens by accident. Even lottery winners have to buy a ticket. Unfortunately for most, they treat true wealth building as something on a long list of financial chores and often it's last on the list. Yes, we all intend to plan for the future but it's always something that is so far off. So we wait. "I'll get around to it" is a famous line that I've heard since I started my career. But when? What will be the precipitating factor? The next change to your career? The hypothetical upcoming change in the stock market that has already disappointed you? The unknown changes in the tax laws? Or the worst of all – significant changes to your health or the health of a loved one? What does it take?

Time marches on, markets rise and fall, taxes change (always have and always will), careers always evolve, and sooner or later people eventually fall ill. Why is it that some people cannot take the initiative, the call to action while others clearly hear and heed the warning? It's all a matter of priorities. Most people, when they become aware of their financial woes, seem to find any reason not to address them regardless of their financial status. Wealthy or not, they go through their mental laundry list of excuses why NOT to address these issues. Problem is, they neglect to consider the most important obligation on the list: THEMSELVES AND, IN TURN, THEIR FAMILIES!

Wealth building and particularly wealth protection is not a luxury, it's a necessity – at least if you don't want to spend your golden years living on social security (and counting on that really is a gamble at best). Growing and protecting your wealth must be treated as a high-priority investment, not an ugly expense. You and your future are important! Nothing, outside of your family, should take a higher priority when it comes to building and protecting your wealth. We've all heard this advice before but "pay yourself first." Why should any entity, company, or person take a higher financial priority?

Currency vs. Wealth

For those of you who may not be aware, let me give you a quick history lesson on currency or paper money in the United States. From the days of the Revolutionary War, the United States often traded precious metals for goods and services and would often create paper currency or certificates that could be traded in for gold or silver at any time. As a result, the dollar became the world's standard currency and the values of many foreign currencies were pegged to the dollar, as was the price of gold ($35/ounce). By law the U.S. Treasury was required to have at least 40% of the paper currency backed by gold. The problem was that many foreign countries took advantage of this law and would often trade in dollars for gold, depleting the U.S. gold reserve and lowering the amount of paper currency the U.S. could legally print.

On August 15, 1971, President Richard Nixon decided to put a stop to this practice and took the U.S. off the "gold standard" which stopped the flow of assets out of the U.S. Unfortunately it also devalued our own currency in the process. Though he was praised for making a necessary adjustment to keep foreign countries from wreaking havoc with our monetary system, the move infused the world markets with a new strain of instability – a floating dollar.

Ever since that time, the dollar has incrementally decreased in value. And yet so many people continue saving and investing with the same mentality as those in pre-1971 America, when the dollar was actually tied to real gold. They continue to practice accumulation theory (review p.21), thinking if they put enough money in the bank and leave it alone it will somehow retain its value. It doesn't. And it's not the source of true wealth. It's not the power that flows through the copper wire. Piles of it do not create value. Currency is a tool of trading which can be lost. Tools are not the same thing as wealth. Value can only come from the use of those tools in a correlated and focused plan. As syndicated columnist Warren Brookes put it, "If we were to destroy every piece of paper currency in the world, and every bank account entry, we would not have destroyed one shred of economic wealth."

So what is true wealth? Wealth is something you can rely on. Wealth exists regardless of market conditions. It weathers price fluctuations and becomes the rock upon which you can build your financial future.

For example, I have a client in his mid-60s who had huge holdings in one of the major banks. I'm talking about significant holdings – 1.5 million shares that were selling at $66 a share at one point in time. Currently they're worth $4.50 a share. Now you tell me, is that wealth? Yes he was wealthy. He still is wealthy, but look at the amount of wealth he lost because he thought currency equaled wealth.

In the interim, he has other holdings of commercial real estate and even if there's a moderate decline, he still has the wealth that's in there. Unlike stock holdings that can fluctuate with every fear and panic in the market, the relative value of his commercial real estate will remain. He also has large amounts of whole life insurance. And when those bank holdings went down, he started accessing the cash value of his life insurance to support his business. Now, I am not saying that real estate alone is the panacea or answer to wealth erosion; it's merely one part of the elephant as is this client's whole life insurance.

Can you see the difference? True Wealth doesn't disappear overnight. Currency does.

Another client fell prey to Bernie Madoff to the tune of $50 million. This classic example shows how expendable currency really is. It's just a tool! Their true wealth actually lies within their real estate holdings. They'll never see that $50 million again, but now they no longer think of money or currency as wealth. They have subsequently purchased very large amounts of life insurance which could not be taken away. You don't have to do a thing to lose currency. It loses value every day thanks to President Nixon and the markets.

The key to Prosperity Economics is building wealth and there is no better way to build wealth than utilizing the right financial tools in the right way at the right time.

Building Confidence – Utilization Theory

Where fear-based scarcity thinking encourages people to hoard and accumulate, prosperity thinking encourages utilization. Going back to Steve D'Annunzio's copper wire analogy – stockpiling mountains of copper wire will not give us more electricity. Only when we properly connect the copper wire and utilize that tool do we get more electricity.

If we want to grow wealth, we can't do it by leaving every penny we've earned in a bank vault or in the stock market. Again, accumulating is not the answer since the value of that tool can change overnight. The tool of currency has to be utilized in an intelligent and clever manner for wealth to grow.

In fact if no one was willing to put their money into circulation via loans, investments, and just plain old transactional business, the economy would collapse overnight. Currency is the lifeblood of the economy and it has to move to energize the financial world – yours and mine.

So what's the best way to utilize your tools (currency) to build true wealth? Utilization theory is not about throwing your money to the winds of the market and hoping for a return. You have to be a smart manager or steward of your tools and resources and it starts with creating the right foundation.

Creating the Foundation

> *"If you always do what you always did,*
> *you'll always get what you always got."*
> **Mark Twain**

Over the last century, change has been the one constant. Yet the more things have changed, the more people resist changing the way they think and behave. Then they get angry or scared with the results. If you want different results you have to…change. At all levels of wealth, large or small, one must have an open mind.

Let's start with a change we could all benefit from – learning from the past. In the past, investing was much more conservative. People invested their money in stable instruments like treasury bills and saving accounts. Then as we reached the "information age" we all abandoned such conservative thinking and chased after the "quick gains" of the stock market. It was a modern-day gold rush where people abandoned the wisdom of the past for the excitement of the future! And despite the vast swings in the market since that time, the see-saw that now creates stomach churning days and nights for even the most sophisticated investors, we have not learned the lesson to be had.

So how do we learn the lessons that are right in front of our eyes and right the financial ship? It's actually a lot simpler than you may think. But you can't be like the blind men who could only consider their own point of view. They were blinded not only by their physical loss of sight but by their own hubris and knowledge which mirrors the situation so many people find themselves in today. There's a great deal of knowledge out there, but knowledge alone can't guide your financial ship or help it chart a safe course through today's troubled international and tax-plagued waters. However there is one tool that, like a compass, can point us in the right direction and it's called the Pyramid of Investments.

The Pyramid of Investments

Speculative
Art
Metals
Gem Stones
Options
Commodities
Oil Exploration
Venture Capital

Conservative
Sale of Covered Options
Conservative Equities
(Utility Stocks, Convertible
Bonds, Balanced Funds)
Residence, GNMA,
Retirement Plans, Corporate
Bonds, Municipal Bonds

U.S. Govt. Notes and Bonds

Equity Partnerships
Investment Real Estate

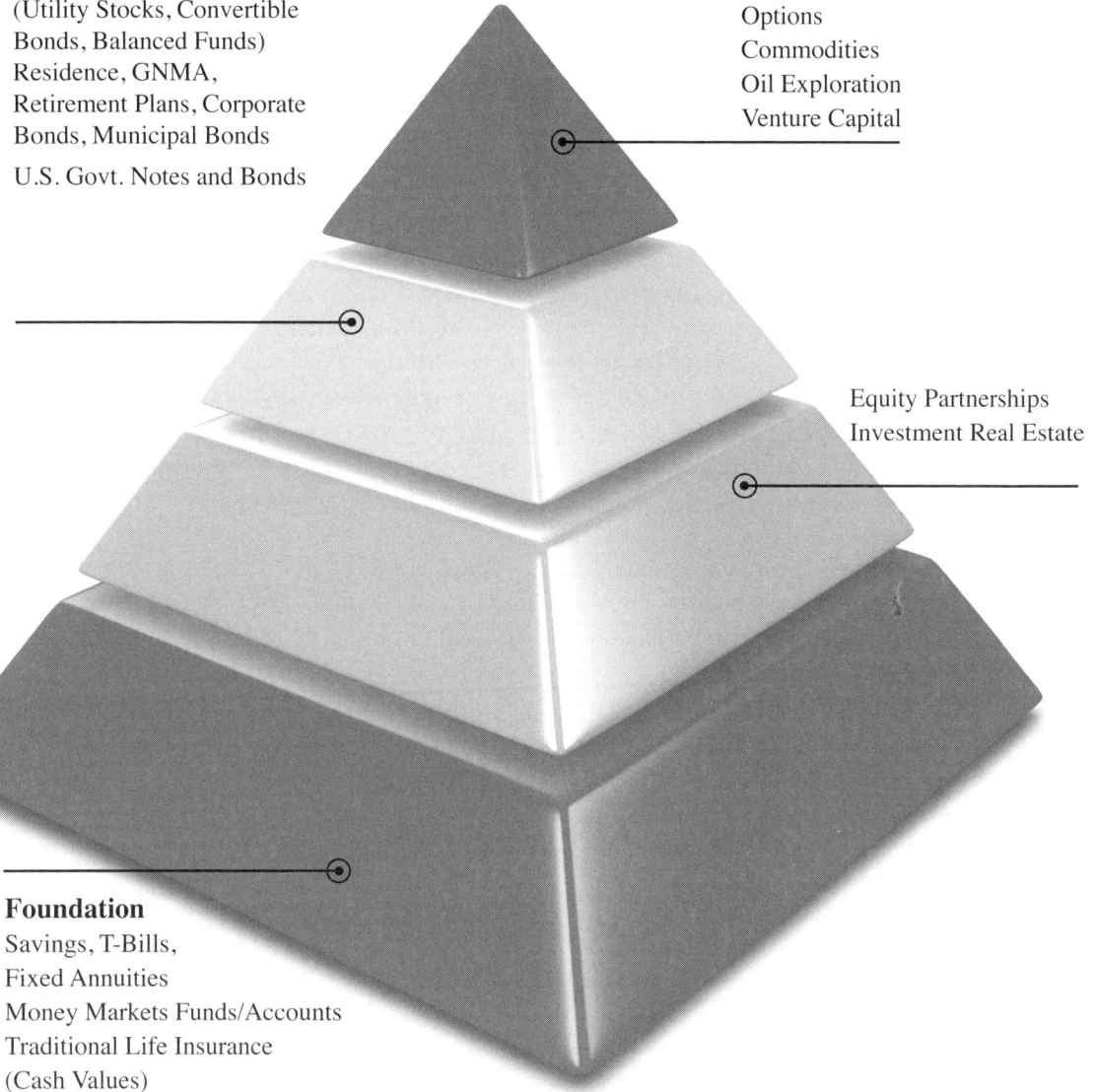

Foundation
Savings, T-Bills,
Fixed Annuities
Money Markets Funds/Accounts
Traditional Life Insurance
(Cash Values)

As you can see, there is nothing new or ground-breaking about this Pyramid. At the bottom we see the "old school" financial instruments like savings accounts, treasury bills (or T-Bills), fixed annuities, money market funds or accounts and traditional full life insurance – you know the one most agents talk you out of in favor of term life insurance so you can lower your monthly premium payments (but at what cost to your future?)

The next level or "growth" level is filled with equity partnerships, investment real estate, growth stocks and mutual funds, variable life insurance and variable annuities. As you can tell this level has a higher level of risk but it's still considered reasonable.

The third tier contains the sale of covered options, conservative equities (such as utility stocks, convertible bonds and balanced funds), your own home residence, GNMA (Government National Mortgage Association or "Ginnie May") bonds, retirement plans, corporate bonds and municipal bonds as well as U.S. government notes and bonds. It's interesting that this tier contains what we commonly consider (or have been taught to consider) the "conservative investments. But conservative by whose standards? Again, there is more risk in this level and it may surprise you that your own home is in this mix, but realize that the value of your home is very much tied to a volatile market and we all know how the housing bubble put a lot of mortgages underwater.

Finally we reach the pinnacle or "speculative" peak of the Pyramid. It's loaded with provocative, high risk investments such as art, precious metals, gem stones, stock options, commodities, oil exploration, and venture capital. This level is loaded with risk. It's at the peak since it points the way to loss. Common sense tells you to avoid these kinds of investments but the thrill of gambling isn't confined to Vegas and Atlantic City and there is never a shortage of investors willing to gamble away their future.

The Tipping Point

Now no one would question the amount of risk in each of these levels or categories. The risk-to-reward can be appropriate in their given levels. Every financial tool can have its proper place at the right point in time. The key to financial success is knowing when it's time to build certain blocks of the Pyramid. To better understand, let's first look at how the world is taught to look at this Pyramid today.

Old School and Boring!
Savings
T-Bills
Fixed Annuities
Money Markets Funds/Accounts
Traditional Life Insurance
(Cash Values)

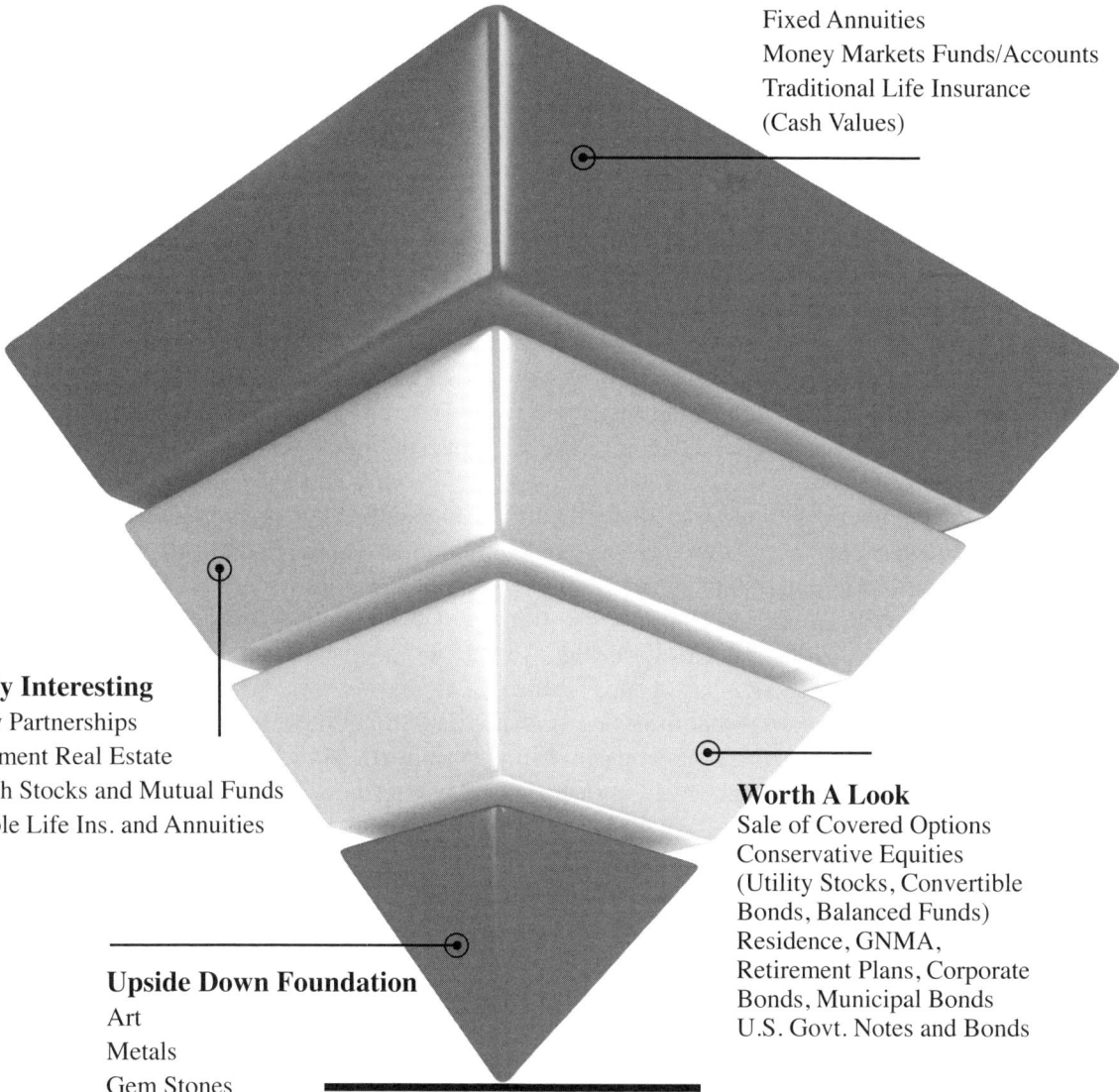

Barely Interesting
Equity Partnerships
Investment Real Estate
Growth Stocks and Mutual Funds
Variable Life Ins. and Annuities

Worth A Look
Sale of Covered Options
Conservative Equities
(Utility Stocks, Convertible
Bonds, Balanced Funds)
Residence, GNMA,
Retirement Plans, Corporate
Bonds, Municipal Bonds
U.S. Govt. Notes and Bonds

Upside Down Foundation
Art
Metals
Gem Stones
Options
Commodities
Oil Exploration
Venture Capital

Notice any differences (and I'm not just talking about the rearrangement of levels)? That's right, the Pyramid is upside down! The "foundation" of the Pyramid is on its point!! We are taught risk first rather than protection first. Stop and think for a moment – if this would work even for a brief time, what is protecting everything inside the Pyramid from the various exposures to erosion such as taxes, inflation, lawsuits or at worst, death? These are some of the most common winds of change we all face.

Do you know anyone who has built anything stable on a point? Oh I'm sure a creative architect could design something to look like it was standing on a small point, but he would also have to hide the elements of a true structural foundation otherwise the Pyramid or one's financial house would collapse. Gravity or the winds of change would bring it crashing down. That's more than just an inconvenient truth, it's a fact. Yet in today's financial world we are very much like the blind men and only see what we want to see. We conveniently ignore the facts for what we perceive to be instant gratification.

What are the facts? Perhaps it's time you asked. Take a look at the financial instruments you currently invest your money in. Where do the majority of your investment dollars go? If you're like most folks, those dollars are going into the stock market in one shape or form. It could be in "qualified" retirement plans such as 401(k)s, profit sharing plans, IRAs, or "professionally" managed non-qualified portfolios or any number of the thousands, yes thousands of myriad investments that have been developed to bring the general public into the market. This is the same fear-inducing stock market that produces wild and unpredictable swings which, in turn, rob people of true wealth.

Consider a so-called "retirement" investment like a 401(k) or any type of retirement fund. Where do the managers of these funds put their money? In the stock market so they can have exposure to growth and eventually have the nest egg they dream of. But can that really be achieved and how can we know when it's the right time to pull out?

What about investing in overseas markets? We live in a global economy where shifts in our markets affect their markets and clearly vice versa as evidenced by the 2012 European economic debt crisis. What will happen to the world economy when the solvent nations of Asia fall upon the same ills? There is no "safe" market. This is another inconvenient fact that many turn a blind eye to.

Unfortunately, our fears are also contagious and now they can spread to the four corners of the earth almost instantly. Everyone everywhere feels the financial tremors. And yet we just keep pumping money into financial instruments that are not truly bearing fruit!

Like the blind men in the story, we only see our part of the elephant and cling to it so tightly that we fail to connect the dots and see the truth. The market is the pinnacle of the Pyramid, the very point on which the economic winds of change can shake the financial world in an instant! It is not a solid foundation upon which you should build your financial house. It's worse than building a house on sand because sand is more solid than a point. A foolish man can build on sand and, for a while, the house will stand. Until storms show up and knock the house financially and literally off point. What can survive that disaster? Nothing!

Today's market weather comes with regular, category five financial hurricanes. How can anything built on a point withstand that kind of storm? The slightest breeze would topple the structure and you'd spend all your effort rebuilding…over and over and over again. That really is the definition of insanity. People keep building on the tip of the Pyramid and hope the results will be different and every time, without fail, it tips and falls. They just keep getting what they've been getting. No wonder they're riddled with fear. No wonder they're paralyzed. Nothing seems to work. And the uncertainty feeds back into the fear creating a firestorm of Scarcity Economics where everyone and everything gets burned.

Everything is in flux. People run from one investment to another chasing the gains they hope to achieve and continuing to fan the flames. Gradually they lose confidence in the fund managers and they move onto the next great scheme, ignoring the dangers and potential losses. They desperately cling to their part of the elephant and live from day to day hoping things will improve. Then when the occasional gain shows up, they're like a gambling addict and decide to spin the financial roulette wheel one more time. It never ends and the hole in the financial soul never heals.

Where can we find financial healing? Where can we find the stability we all crave inside? Where are the financial safe harbors? It all begins with a solid foundation (you know that "old school" stuff at the base of the original Pyramid).

Slow and Steady *vs*. Get Rich Quick

So you've seen the Pyramid of Investments. You've learned the dangers of building on the tip. That realization alone gives you a leg up on a solid financial future. You may even think that building on the "old school" foundation might be a good idea. It seems like good common sense. But you still have to unlearn what you've been taught. You still have to overcome the dirty windows of your own paradigm blindness but you have to be patient.

Patience has always been a prerequisite for building a protective foundation for wealth. But today's market calls like a siren as its beautiful strains lure us into thinking we can bypass more stable investment vehicles and reach the golden shores of financial prosperity in a few quick leaps. Only when we're in the middle of our leap do we realize that we've just launched ourselves directly at the rocks of financial ruin.

No one needs to suffer such economic destruction if they can learn to resist the enticements of pundits and their misinformation. In my experience, following their direction leaves almost as much behind in ruins as it purports to build for the future, regardless of how much wealth one has.

Solid Financial Footing

Every good structure just like every good plan needs a solid foundation if you want it to stand for any length of time. Most structures are built using a concrete foundation with reinforced steel, but the best foundations are often found on hillsides where structures must be able to withstand the forces of gravity that can pull a building down the hill during heavy rains or natural disasters like an earthquake.

Some builders think such events will rarely happen and they just go about building a standard concrete foundation and keep doing what they've always done, feeling it will be enough, and it may be.

But builders who design structures to withstand any calamity sink caissons deep into earth until they reach bedrock. Then no matter what storms or disasters occur, the foundation of the structure is solid as the rock it's anchored to.

Likewise, we need a solid financial foundation to build true wealth. It may or may not be fast, but building your financial foundation solidly and carefully will actually enable you to take on a few riskier ventures further down the road.

Buckets of Wealth

With a firm foundation in place, it's time to build what I like to call "buckets of wealth." Buckets of wealth are any financial vehicles that are recognized as untouchable by Uncle Sam or the fickle market swings, vehicles that give a guaranteed growth rate with tax leverage. Buckets of wealth are financial tools or instruments that act as safe harbors when the economic storms take their toll as they often do. These are also truly diversified strategies that keep your nest eggs in a number of baskets unlike most "diversified" funds that all use the same info to invest in the same stocks and bonds. Buckets of wealth also give you a permission slip to live life to the fullest – even in retirement!

The (Unknown) Permission Slip

Retirement is a relative term. It's not the same for everyone. Each stage of financial security changes the interpretation of what retirement might mean to an individual. Regardless of the level of one's financial security, no one wants to run out of money before they die. Yet that is one of the greatest fears that most people experience as they move closer to retirement age, even for the affluent. The specter of interest rate fluctuations, real estate value depression, credit tightening, personal inflation, and tax increases looms larger with each passing year. Maintenance on your home or vehicles take a chunk of your nest egg and, god forbid, you encounter any kind of a health issue. What if you realize that your nest egg, no matter how large it may appear, may not be enough to continue living life at a level of comfort you're accustomed to? Your future doesn't seem so golden anymore and you can't seem to put away retirement funds fast enough.

Enter the concept of the "Permission Slip." What is a "Permission Slip"? If you've created these financial safety nets I call buckets of wealth, then you have created "permission" to be more aggressive with your retirement and other investment dollars. You no longer have to worry about losing your nest egg and can be totally focused on growing all your assets!

Understanding and employing the concept of a "Permission Slip" allows you the affordability to be more aggressive with all of your investment portfolios during your asset growth stage. During your asset distribution stages a "Permission Slip" allows you to be living in your money versus living on your money. We are taught that living on interest only is the way to go versus living on principal and interest in the proper way to distribute assets. A "Permission Slip" also alleviates the interest rate fluctuations the economy endures. Lastly, it reduces all forms of taxation including income and ultimately estate taxation.

Now you have "permission" to employ wealth replacement strategies and, combined with other assets, it allows you to breathe easy knowing you and your loved ones are taken care of from a protection and growth perspective. Guaranteed.

Seeing the Whole Elephant

So how do you build true wealth? If you look at the Pyramid of Investments, the first level or base of the Pyramid is really about wealth. It's nothing exotic. It's everything that's solid that cannot be taken away. In 2008, money markets dipped below dollar-to-dollar net asset value. So if you had $100,000 and it fell down to .98 cents, you had $98,000, which was not the concept of a money market account. But it's still safer than being in the stock market. People say bonds will never default, but we don't know. Orange County, California defaulted, didn't they?

More than anything you have to see the whole elephant because a holistic approach allows for change. We all live and breathe change on a daily basis, yet those who plan for change by creating buckets of wealth are able to stabilize and protect their precious investments. The stock market is a roller coaster you cannot control. You can't stabilize it or the bond market.

As I stated earlier, we're now in an international economy where all markets are volatile and subject to the challenges each nation faces. It started in the late 80s and as global communications grew, so did our financial interdependence. You have to create asset stabilization models with floors – whether it's a retirement plan, an estate plan, or a business agreement. There has to be a well-constructed strategy in place for each "what if?" scenario. Regardless of what takes place in the economy, it's always the same approach. That's how buckets of wealth protect you. When one asset dips, another increases and offsets the dip.

Of course stabilizing assets is essential to establishing a solid financial foundation. Picture a house with just the 2 x 4s stuck in the ground not nailed together or on top of a concrete slab or a basement. What would happen when the winds of change would come? It would blow right over, just like the upside down Pyramid we looked at earlier. And that's what's been happening in the United States and the rest of the world, more so now than ever because of our global economy.

So it really is back to the fundamentals of creating a foundation for your financial home first. The idea of the Pyramid of Investments is to start building wealth and then the currency comes. You have to build wealth from the ground up not from the tip up. It's an organic growth vs. a get-rich-quick scheme.

People are not being taught the way money truly works, about how wealth is truly created. If you go back to the 1950s and 1960s, the stock market was available for a far lesser number of people than it is today. There were no 401(k)s, IRAs, day traders, or discount on line wire houses. People created wealth using brick-and-mortar financial tools and protected them before moving on to the next level in their lives. Ignoring and not implementing these basic tenants is the sign of a blind man that cannot see the whole elephant. And seeing the whole elephant is not just important, it's critical when it comes to creating financial security.

Chapter 4

The Life Cycle Wealth Management Process™

Now that your eyes are open and you can see the whole elephant, it's time to take steps toward creating a financial plan of action that will ensure you never fall back to the dark side of Scarcity Economics. It's time to put prosperity thinking to work for you.

Good plans don't just appear at the touch of a financial planner's magic wand. They also don't happen overnight. And to create an effective plan you have to understand the process. Each plan is a unique creation that must change as the winds of change blow.

Product vs. Process

Most people want to be into the stock market but the stock market is not the only place to be into. The stock market, bonds, home mortgages, retirement plans, life insurance – how do they all interact together? There are direct correlations between them. Nobody addresses the fact that assets have to interact with each other in order for them to perform optimally. Your assets are not separate animals. They are part of the same animal – your financial elephant. To plan around one asset class without looking at creating a foundation and long term interaction between asset classes is worse than being blind, it's irresponsible. Too many financial planners do just that because that's what they are taught. They offer micro-economic plans rather than macro-economic plans. Is this wrong? It is if they ignore the needs of the client.

Every client is different with different needs and situations. No two are exactly alike and yet many advisors utilize a one-size-fits-all philosophy when it comes to creating a plan. It's a problem I call Product vs. Process.

People are always looking at products. They are coerced into taking the Pyramid of Investments and turning it upside down. "Let's get into the stock market," they say, "Let's get into that get-rich-quick product!" without understanding the correlation between all of their assets. Mortgages are true tax deductions. Qualified retirement plans are true tax deferrals because you (or your heirs) do have to pay the tax sooner or later. So you have to recognize – do you want deferrals today or deductions today or a combination of the two? They both have their places but understanding the differences initially and planning for each in the long term is imperative.

Can you see how critical it can be to coordinate your assets? Failing to plan can cost you a bundle and when you're planning for financial success, no one has money to burn. You need a process to address the ever-changing nature of your financial landscape. "Failing to plan is planning to fail" – a saying that was coined in the 1990s still rings true today.

Most people have a variety of assets and tools. They have retirement plans, homes, mortgages (or they may not have mortgages), insurance and investments. They think that the stock market is the darling of the world without realizing the stock market is quite literally legalized gambling. They may have bond portfolios. They may have life insurances. They may have disability and their long-term care. Yet none of it is structured in a coordinated method. None of it.

It's like having a football team where everyone knows their function or role, but there's no quarterback. There is no one to huddle with the players so they can coordinate their play. So when the ball is snapped, everyone does their job but nothing is accomplished. In fact some players may actually bump into each other as they duplicate the efforts of other players. Not every player needs to run with the ball. Not every player needs to block. So, on the financial playing field, you end up with plans that can never really score the big win for their owners and may actually cause the team to lose ground.

Recognizing that the financial plans need a quarterback to call the plays and coordinate the players or assets, I created the Life Cycle Wealth Management Process. Notice I didn't call it the Life Cycle

Wealth Management **Plan** because it's more than a plan. A plan is good for one play. But when things change on the playing field, you have to adjust your overall game plan and that is a process. In the game of life it's an ongoing process that changes with the needs of the client and it coordinates the assets of the clients to give them the maximum benefit regardless of the season of life they are currently in.

Eliminate Lost Opportunity Costs

One thing the Life Cycle Wealth Management Process protects you against is lost opportunities to grow your wealth. For example, there are many people who might advise you to pay off your home loans early to save interest. Sounds like a sound principle, right? If you did this, you'd lose your tax deduction on the mortgage interest to one extent or another, right? And since you decided to pay off the loan early, the bank uses the money you just gave them to make more loans and generate more money for themselves. The concept is simple yet difficult for many to accept. Pay off your mortgage and you're debt free – the American dream! But what if you need to get at the equity that is locked up in the house? Can you? In today's day and age, it is no longer an easy task to access that asset, if at all.

Perhaps we are again living in the past. Yes, our parents lived in a time when their real estate holdings were indeed assets. They purchased them and years later they were worth 10 times, 20 times, 30 times what they paid for their homes or real estate. But look at the real estate bubble that the banks created in the late 2000s. How many millions of people jumped into the real estate market, commercial or residential, as yet another get-rich-quick scheme? Flipping became all the rage. Now, how many of those same people have little left to their names? This is not to say that owning real estate is a negative financial strategy, quite contrary. It's more about where and when is the right time and proper structure of ownership. It all comes back to understanding the Pyramid of Investments.

If you look at all your assets and coordinate them, you can avoid lost opportunity costs and grow your wealth in ways you may not even be aware of yet. There is so much opportunity to grow! But you also have to be willing to protect your wealth.

Stopping the Wealth Vultures

Another benefit of the Life Cycle Wealth Management Process is protection against loss. Wealth vultures are always nearby and more than willing to siphon off your wealth at the drop of a hat. The first step in stopping them is to recognize what they are and how they impact your bottom line.

TAXES

Death and taxes are the two constants in this world of ours and while death is certain, taxes can and should be minimized. Failing to take advantage of certain tax regulations is a sad, sad state of affairs and can cost you more than you'll know. A good plan recognizes this vulture and finds legal ways to reduce taxes. Taxes are not a form of social philanthropy and paying more than you're legally required is a costly error in judgment. Learn to be smart and use the laws to your advantage.

INFLATION

As the dollar loses value, the prices of goods and services rises. Inflation is inevitable and there is no way to predict when it will hit and how hard. As I write this book, the world faces potential economic meltdown because of unabashed governmental spending. Sure, it's politically "correct" to print money and spend it where it appears to be needed but is it fiscally prudent? Trillions of dollars, trillions of Euros today can only mean higher if not hyperinflation in the future. So you must create buckets of true wealth as a protection against such a swift vulture.

MARKET SWINGS

The market giveth and the market taketh away. It's a never ending cycle that no one can really predict and a wealth vulture can be hard to dodge. You can watch the trends and base your decisions on those facts but who can see things like Lehman Brothers collapsing and taking the whole market down with it? Worse part is people are becoming complacent about today's uncanny volatility. I can't state how many times I hear people say "Oh, the markets' down but it will pop back up. It always does." People seem to forget 1927, 1982, 1987, 2008, 2011! Once again, building solid financial safety nets may save the day when the markets take their next plunge.

LAWSUITS

Lawsuits are one of the most common wealth vultures. Success is like a beacon to them and they come in flocks to fleece your wealth. Even if you feel your income and investments are relatively small, lawsuits swoop in and snatch wealth from just about everyone. You don't have to be a billionaire to give someone an excuse to sue. Knowing this, it's critical that you structure your assets in such a way as to make them virtually immune to lawsuits and claims.

CREDITORS

If you're having a dispute with a creditor, don't be surprised if they go after your assets. This wealth vulture is much more common than you think and you have to make sure your nest egg is secure against any possible claims.

The Boy Scouts have a motto: Be Prepared. These wealth vultures, like many others, can be neutralized if you prepare properly.

Taking Control

There is only one way to avoid the wealth vultures and that is to create a coordinated process. Without such a process, you're much like Alice who found herself lost in Wonderland:

"Would you tell me, please, which way I ought to go from here?"

"That depends a good deal on where you want to get to," said the Cat.

"I don't much care where--" said Alice.

"Then it doesn't matter which way you go," said the Cat.

"... so long as I get SOMEWHERE," Alice added as an explanation.

"Oh, you're sure to do that," said the Cat, "if you only walk long enough."

(Lewis Carroll, Alice's Adventures in Wonderland)

Alice was sure to get somewhere if she walked long enough, and that's the approach most people take with their money. They think if they work long and hard enough, they'll be wealthy and live their golden years in comfort and style. How many people today realize that they cannot have those golden years they dreamed of? Without a coordinated plan of action you will fall victim to self-serving peddlers of products, lost opportunities and wealth vultures that can reduce your wealth to financial bones. The Life Cycle Wealth Management Process will enable you to prevail against all of these pitfalls and more.

Connecting the Dots

As I said earlier, you need a quarterback to coordinate the process of financial planning and a good quarterback connects the dots. As he lines up to take the snap, he quickly surveys the defense and may decide to change the play. He knows how all the positions and players may interact and makes adjustments that he knows will allow his team to succeed.

Financial planning should be no different and the key to connecting the dots is understanding the Four Quadrants and how they impact one another.

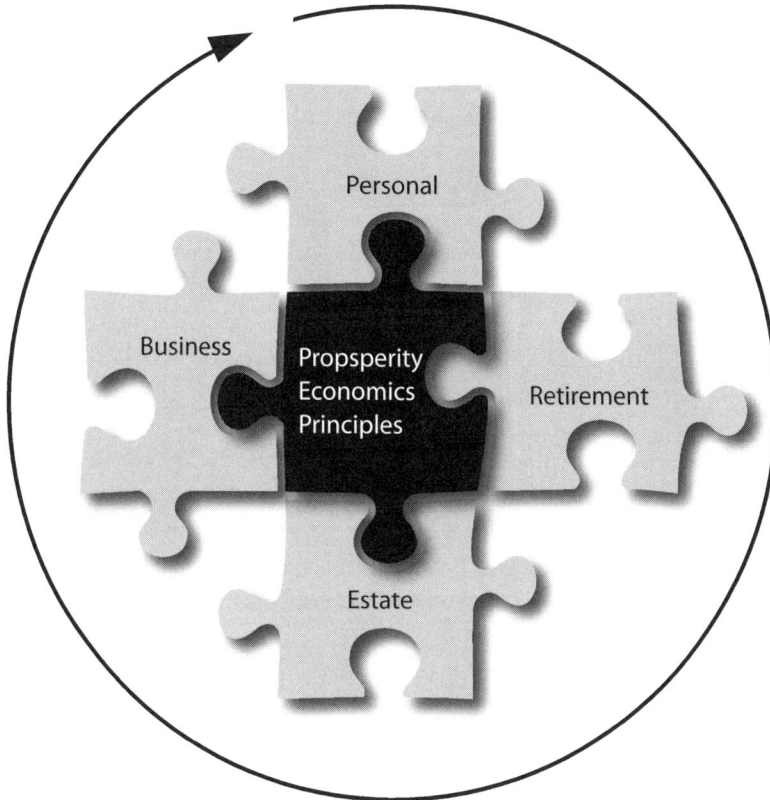

The Four Quadrants

Business, Personal, Estate, Retirement

As you can see from the diagram, your financial process needs to address four separate areas of your life: Business, Personal, Retirement, and Estate.

Business is a vital quadrant of planning. Whether you own a business, work as a consultant, or are employed by someone else, everyone needs to address their employment now and in the future. If you own a business and have partners, you are planning to protect the business and in turn your families. If you don't have partners, you may choose to leave your business to your children, in which case you want a plan that allows you to exit the business and help your children successfully step into the business. You also need to develop contingency strategies to protect you and everything you've worked for from being sidetracked or even destroyed by unexpected misfortune.

The goal, whether you are a sole owner or there are multiple owners of a business, is to structure your succession planning in such a way that it acknowledges the concerns in the other quadrants instead of blindly creating a plan that may unintentionally cause harm or loss.

The Personal quadrant addresses your personal goals and concerns. It encompasses everything in your personal life. After all, everything we do in all the other quadrants should maximize what we have emotionally and financially in our Personal Quadrants. For example, a business owner is in business to create wealth. Ultimately the wealth is personal wealth which allows you to pursue more personal interests.

Retirement is self-explanatory. It deals with the future (or in some cases very near future) and whenever you plan for the future you always have to consider the impact today's choices have on your tomorrows. And you have to ask the right questions. Do you have enough money to retire? What do you want out of retirement? What's the lifestyle you want?

Finally, your Estate quadrant is all about the legacy you build and leave to your family. You must structure that quadrant in such a way that you minimize taxes and leave the most wealth you possibly can to your loved ones while retaining control over your assets.

Through all the quadrants, you also need to employ the strategy of asset stabilization by using the buckets of wealth I mentioned in the previous chapter (see p.43). This strategy gives you assets that are guaranteed to increase when other assets may be decreasing, leveling out the financial dips and bumps in the cycles of life.

These four quadrants, whether you recognize it or not, are very closely knit together. Your retirement plan ties into your business plan. Your business plan ties into your retirement distribution plan. Your retirement distribution plan ties into your estate plan. Your business plan ties into your estate plan. They're all very closely intertwined and until you see how they impact each other, you could be basing crucial decisions on information gleaned from the observations of a blind man on one side of the elephant. Talk about the blind leading the blind!

The Life Cycle Wealth Management Process connects the dots and takes into account all of the Four Quadrants and how they interact with one another.

It creates a bridge over life and ties all the cycles of your life into a singular plan to help you maximize wealth accumulation, minimize risk, and anticipate crucial end-of-life estate decisions. Best of all, it is centered on the Principles of Prosperity Economics which frees you from the fear-based decisions of the past and allows you to chart a new course to wealth.

Characteristics of an Ideal Financial Plan

Growing wealth isn't easy, but one thing that can simplify the process is having a process in place that encompasses all the best characteristics of an ideal financial plan. And while I'm not so naïve as to think there is a perfect plan, I do think the best plans share a number of common characteristics.

A systemic flow of money into the plan – While currency is tool, it is the flow of money that helps create wealth when it's part of a plan. Don't confuse this with accumulation theory. We're not talking about creating piles of money, but creating a flow of money. It's much more dynamic and, in turn, helps to create more wealth. Sitting in a bank it only accumulates dust and a whopping 1% return. Factor in a few wealth vultures like inflation and you're actually losing money. Need I say more?

A guaranteed return on the money – If your current plan can't give you a guaranteed return on your money, then why would you continue funding it? No one wants to gamble with their nest egg. A guaranteed return is one of those buckets of wealth that allow you an upside of growth.

Availability of the money when needed – What good is money if you can't access it in a time of need? Most people have a 401(k) with a small match. Let's say someone has $500,000 in their 401(k). The most they can borrow is 50% of that up to $50,000. That's not availability of the money when it's needed. It's a cap and then you have to repay it with after-tax dollars. So you're being double-taxed on it. You want your money to be available without penalty when you need it.

Minimum or no taxes on the accumulation of the money – What good is currency if the return on your investment goes right back out the door to Uncle Sam? While paying taxes cannot be avoided, paying more than required by law is counterproductive.

There are a number of ways to grow wealth while avoiding taxes. Retirement plans are great tools. You just have to know when to implement them in the Pyramid, why you want to implement them, and ultimately how to distribute them with minimal taxes on those retirement accounts.

Ultimately your wealth will be taxed. What you have to do is circumvent that taxation that may come fifty years down the road while you're young enough to make those adjustments and plans.

Minimum or no taxes on the distribution of the money – Again, when you take money out you want to minimize the taxes that are taken. Many don't think about a qualified retirement plan's growth with deferred taxes account. But one must ask throughout – "What will the tax bracket be when I take the money out"? Certainly looking at our national situation today, we are facing higher taxes sooner or later.

Ease of distribution of the money when you want it –Simply put, when do you want the money out? Once you have an answer to that question, you can use a distribution plan that achieves that goal.

Self-Completing Savings Plan – Should anything happen to you and your ability to earn an income, you need assets that will continue to bring in money and fund other parts of your overall plan. No one likes to consider the worst case scenario (except maybe lawyers) but you need contingencies for any interruption to your plan due to death, disability, emergencies or unforeseen factors such as inflation, deflation, or hyperinflation (which we very well may face one day).

Eliminate the potential loss of the money due to market fluctuation – Most plans lose money because their foundation is the tip of the upside down Pyramid of Investments. You have to turn the Pyramid right side up and build a solid foundation. Seems simple but so many people get it wrong and they pay the price. Literally.

Flexibility to change the plan – It's imperative to have flexibility. You absolutely have to realize that a financial plan is a living, breathing, changing plan, year-to-year. Case in point: We had a prominent law firm that (because of the downturn in the economy) came to us. They had a defined benefit plan and a 401(k). The economy had slowed so much that we actually had to distribute some of the plan's assets to stay above water.

They just informed us that they're filing for bankruptcy. So their assets are protected luckily because they're in a qualified plan. Although they can't fund it currently, we have the flexibility to change that plan around and they're still protected.

You have to have flexibility because things change. Maybe all you need is a slight adjustment from year to year but a few degrees of change can make all the difference in your path to creating wealth. I'm sure a few degrees to port would have made all the difference for the Titanic.

Money is free from wealth vultures – Wealth vultures are always lurking and nobody thinks about this. They are always ready to take and spend your money and often they siphon it away just a little at a time – a percentage here, an unnecessary insurance coverage there – but they drain your assets. If you've got a mutual fund, a stock, a bond – is it free from creditors? Only if it's in a trust or qualified plan. Own it on the outside and it's not free from creditors or lawsuit. A good plan recognizes the threats in advance before they strike.

Planning with the Process

So exactly how does the Process work? In the first step or stage of the Life Cycle Wealth Management Process you look at everything you have and I mean everything – every asset, every liability, every business, every piece of real estate, any situation that might impact the bottom line. You don't want to be a blind man and only address the individual parts of the Elephant. You have to connect the dots and see how each part of the financial picture is affected by the other parts as a whole.

With step two you take a look at what is not working. Then in step three, you coordinate all of your assets. Step four is the creation of an effective distribution plan for retirement. Finally, in the fifth step you create an estate plan.

Sounds simple enough, but nothing involving money (and the emotions tied to it) is ever that simple. It's not something you come up with in a day. You're planning for a lifetime and everything has to be considered.

For example – I was meeting with a new client. He and his wife are both professionals. Through his work he has a cash balance plan. He had some life insurance and he has dysfunctional investments so he's down some 22% on the investment end. He also has commercial properties with a debt that's upside down right now. He and his wife make about $2 million a year between the two of them and they have several children. Real estate taxes are upwards of $125,000/year and they're in their mid-forties. Coordinating all this was a puzzle for him.

We installed a defined benefit plan for him (we saved him taxes there) from his private practice. As I said, he had a cash balance plan elsewhere at another practice. That's awfully top-heavy when it comes to retirement dollars. So what we're doing now is re-allocating the retirement dollars. We're leaving those contributions going in because you never want to give up a tax deduction. Whenever you have a deferral or a deduction, you always want to take advantage of that because there's a lost opportunity cost on giving up a deferral or a deduction. So we want to take those deferrals and deductions.

He's actually so deeply involved in the qualified planning world that now we're starting to take assets and reallocate assets to the non-qualified world. Why? Because the concept of a retirement plan is essentially to retire in a lower tax bracket than you're in today. Unfortunately, we in the retirement planning world know that will not be the case. What will be the case? We don't know. We don't know what's going to happen with taxes. We can only presume they're not going to go down. They're only going to go up. That means we have to have a defensive stance.

So this guy is putting away some $125,000 a year into his retirement plan and his wife is putting away $22,000 a year into her retirement plan. That's a lot of money going into retirement plans when they're both fairly young. So what we're did is make a projection based on a simple, linear 4% growth, and that 4% growth turned out to be X amount of dollars in the end.

We know it's going to change just based on the projections. That's why any kind of plan has to be a living, breathing thing. It is not set in stone. They change all the time. His expenses today with his children are going to be entirely different once his kids go to college or get married. So we're reviewing how to get them more non-retirement dollars.

We're also looking at their debt and working with their accountant and their attorney. From the accounting side we're looking at – how do we structure this debt? He's got $30,000 a month in mortgage payments and taxes.

So we looked at ways to restructure so we can minimize the debt. It may involve paying off or selling some of the properties (because some of them are rental properties that are just under water) and then move them forward where they have higher cash flow. In this kind of case if they have an attorney they want to work with (they did), we will work with the attorney to help them coordinate their assets.

That's a classic example of how the Life Cycle Wealth Management Process works.

So what these people did in the personal sector – they took that Pyramid of Investments and they did it upside down. They set it on the pinnacle, not the base. The reason? They wanted to live in a $5 million home. They live in a $5 million home but it has them strapped. They wanted to be in the stock market. They're in the stock market but they're panic-stricken about their non-retirement and their retirement dollars. So they're subject to all kinds of fluctuation and Scarcity Economics is driving their decisions.

Being professionals, one of the biggest problems they never thought of is asset protection, to start an interplay of protected assets – buckets of wealth.

So that is a classic example of the Pyramid turned upside down and how it was hurting some very successful people. By the end of the year, they will be set up entirely differently. Their debts will be reduced and their cash flow will climb. We're also doing a cash flow analysis on them to see how to create even more wealth.

Ultimately what we'll end up doing is tying their assets into a variety of trusts for the children to prevent any estate taxation.

A Living, Breathing Plan

Even though we've spend a lot of time with our clients, I know we'll continue to make course corrections and adjustments as their lives unfold. Sadly, I often find people who have spent far too much money investing in plans that were created years ago and never changed. Remember "If it ain't broke, don't fix it"? It's easier for them to think this way. But in reality, the world changes and every plan develops weaknesses somewhere that need to be addressed.

Each stage of life presents its own set of challenges. Managing and protecting your wealth doesn't have to be one of them. Times change, economies change and so should your plan. No one should be a victim of poor planning, ignored changes, or bad advice.

Your plan should be more than just a series of financial products and transactions; it should transform and change with each cycle of life! You need financial planning that continually prepares you for your life's different stages. That's why I developed a living, breathing process to grow wealth – the Life Cycle Wealth Management Process. It's all about protecting people, their business, their families and ultimately to protect their loved ones. Is anything more important?

Chapter 5

Choosing Certainty

"Change is inevitable. Growth is optional."
Walt Disney

Life is filled with choices and, make no mistake, you always have a choice. Some choices may not be pleasant, like deciding whether you should go to the dentist for that aching tooth of yours (either way there's some pain involved). Some choices are much more pleasant like deciding to vacation in Bora Bora or Paris. No matter what your circumstance, we all must make choices and what we choose often determines the course of our lives. If you are not happy with the results of your choices then isn't it time for something different?

The world is gambling with their money hoping that it will reveal a new path to wealth, but the path to wealth has always been paved with certainty, not luck. It's no accident. It's a product of intentional choice. No one can control the financial markets. No one can control the decisions of a large bureaucracy like the IRS. No one can control inflation, but we can control how we grow and protect our wealth.

We don't have to build our financial house on the tip of the Pyramid of Investments. We can build up from a solid foundation that will allow us grow our wealth and protect our future. We can choose Prosperity Economics over the unrealistic fears of Scarcity Economics. We can choose the way of wealth creation. It's all a choice. And now you can make a choice with windows that are crystal clear and no longer clouded by misinformation.

Blind No More

"The first step towards change is awareness."
Nathaniel Branden

They say if you fail to plan, you plan to fail. However if you create a plan using the narrow scope of the blind men, you may very well end up with a financial blueprint built on the upside down Pyramid of Investments. I've seen it happen. The one sure thing it will produce is frustration, fear, and loss. It's time for a change and change begins with awareness.

You no longer have to balance on a board across a pool of imagined financial ruin. Now you recognize fear for what it is: False Evidence Appearing Real. Relying on the pundits and celebrity experts with their wealth of misinformation and opinion will soon be a thing of the past. You realize that money is not wealth but a tool that should be utilized to grow wealth, instead of accumulating in a bank vault where it loses value.

Slow and steady growth is your new goal not the get-rich-quick schemes of the market players. Protecting your financial house through buckets of true wealth is your new strategy, a tactic that will allow you the "permission" to seek out growth and dodge the wealth vultures of taxes, inflation, market swings, lawsuits, and creditors. Best of all you recognize the need to coordinate your assets so they interact in a way that will grow wealth for you and your loved ones.

Your eyes are finally open! You see the whole economic elephant for yourself and just knowing this has created a huge paradigm shift to a new way of thinking, a way no longer ruled by fears, the way of prosperity and peace of mind.

The Path to Prosperity

The path to prosperity is not as elusive as some might think. You've already taken the first step in changing how you think, but knowledge alone is not enough. Prosperity requires wisdom. Does that mean you have to know everything to be wise? Of course not. What it does require is a combination of knowledge and experience.

That's why I say prosperity is the ability to apply wisdom to create value in any context. So it doesn't matter what that context is. If the markets collapsed tomorrow we'd still be able to use wisdom and in turn create value. We could still implement the plans we designed, make the changes required pursuant to whatever is occurring in the world and still find success relative to who we are and what we want. In other words, we can create plans that are impervious to external factors that could destroy us financially.

The smartest people are the ones who realize that they can't be experts at everything. So if you lack financial expertise, you need to seek out someone who has the wisdom to help guide your investment strategies and financial plans – preferably someone who is not mired in scarcity thinking and the fear-based decision making that it breeds. Don't settle for less than a practitioner of Prosperity Economics. Your future and the future of your family is at stake.

Living An Exceptional Life

Whether you enjoy an average life or an exceptional life all depends on who you choose to listen to. If you listen to most of the blind men around the elephant, they'll tell you that wealth is created in the stock market. If that's true why did the recent Facebook IPO lose 31% of its value in 5 days? Does that sound like wealth creation to you? And when the nation's biggest bank, JP Morgan, initially revealed that it lost $2 billion in failed credit default swaps and some 60 days later the number was up to $5.8 billion. It should be easy to see that the odds will never be in the blind men's favor whether they're gambling in Vegas or Wall Street. This is not the path to prosperity.

If you listen to a financial advisor who sees the whole elephant, your chances at living an exceptional life increase significantly. Such an advisor creates a financial plan that connects the dots of their client's unique situation.

Everyone is different and each plan should reflect that. Though it employs a process, an ideal plan is never a cookie-cutter solution. It addresses the needs of each quadrant of a client's life: business, personal, retirement, and estate.

A holistic advisor recognizes each quadrant and how the assets in each quadrant affect one another. They are constantly seeking to protect their client's investments from market meltdowns and wealth vultures alike and they create flexible, living plans that transform to accommodate changes in the life of their client and his or her family. Clients with such an advisor don't need to panic at the first sign of economic peril. They know their advisor has their financial back and will make adjustments to counter any possible situation. Best of all, they can sleep at night. That, all by itself, can make for a pretty exceptional life.

So how do you find such an advisor? To use a sports analogy, you scout the available players.

Finding a Good Quarterback

No one wants to be on a losing team. We all want to be part of a winning tradition and that starts with finding the right players. There are plenty of financial planners, attorneys, and CPAs that will be happy to advise you on how to arrange your financial affairs. So how do you find the best players for each position on the team? You scout. You look at all the available players and try to find an athlete that knows the game, has experience, and has a work ethic and character you can rely on. This is especially important when it comes to hiring a quarterback.

A good quarterback is an essential piece of a championship team. Though he often gets a lot of the fame when things go right, he also takes most of the blame when things go wrong. He is responsible for leading his team and relaying the plays as they're called in by the coach. He has to know every play and what each player is assigned to do. And when he encounters a unique situation on the field, he may change the play.

This is not a job you want to trust to some armchair quarterback you just met at a local sports bar. You want a proven leader with experience, talent, and the intelligence to change the call when needed. It takes millions of dollars to bankroll a professional football team and no owner or coach is going to hire a new quarterback on a whim. They will assess every available player to find the very best quarterback possible. You should do the same when it comes to your financial advisors.

Do your due diligence in finding an advisor who can lead you to victory on the financial playing field. You need someone who can connect the dots, who knows all the variables and how they interact. Your financial quarterback should be someone with that unique combination of knowledge and experience. Remember the formula?

KNOWLEDGE + EXPERIENCE = WISDOM

Your advisor needs to be the embodiment of wisdom, not someone trying to balance your portfolio on the tip of the Pyramid of Investments. Go with a quarterback who is both knowledgeable and has the experience to guide your financial strategies in every arena, be it personal, business, retirement or estate planning.

In the arena of financial planning, no one has to lose. Though each situation may be different, everyone can win if they are willing to choose prosperity and seek out a proven advisor to guide their efforts. The decision is yours. Choose wisely.

If you liked what you've read in this book and think the Life Cycle Wealth Management Process might be something you'd like to explore further, please contact Richard Pope at (516) 677-6212.